MEMORIES OF
NORTHAMPTON

Part of the
MEMORIES *series*

Contents

First published in Great Britain by True North Books Limited, England HX3 6SN. 01422 244555

www.truenorthbooks.com | Copyright © True North Books Limited, 2019

Printed and Bound by Short Run Press Ltd, Exeter.

Text, design and origination by True North Books

Part of the 'Memories' compact series and based on the original Memories of Northampton publication.

Memories are made of this...

Welcome to 'Memories of Northampton - Nostalgia Square', a perfectly packaged look back on some of the places, events and people in the town which have shaped the lives of local people over a period of around half a century.

In page after page of nostalgic images the book gives readers an entertaining glimpse back through the years at how people used to shop, work and play in the days that seem like only yesterday.

Nostalgia is always such a mixture of feelings... We hope that the collection of pictures in this book will remind you of happy days in bygone eras - and who knows, you might even have been there when one of the photographs was taken!

Happy memories!

Around the Town Centre

It is a fairly quiet time of day in the Market Square sometime in the 1950s. Some of the names on the buildings would have been familiar enough at this time, from Roses Fashion Centre and Phoenix Assurance in the rear, to Pearl Assurance and Liptons to the right. In the middle distance, the striking tower of All Saints Church dominates the skyline. Nevertheless, with the square clear of stalls, the eye is inevitably drawn to the focal point, the magnificent fountain on its plinth at the centre. This was made locally and presented to the town in 1863 by Samuel Isaacs to commemorate the marriage of Albert Edward, Prince of Wales, to Princess Alexandra of Denmark.

A modest sized petrol tanker (by modern standards) is rumbling its way across South Bridge and its appearance, linked with the style of the other vehicles on view, would place this photograph as no later than the 1950s. Some interesting buildings are on view including, in the distance, the two breweries of P Phipps & Co and the Northamptonshire Brewery Company. The tall building just beyond the petrol tanker has the inscription EAGLE FOUNDRY just below the triangular pediment. This was originally Rice's Foundry.

Marefair in the 1950s presents a rather gloomy and wet scene but it preserves an image that would otherwise only exist in memory. The whole of the north or left-hand side has been developed into the massive Barclaycard complex, but the imposing structure in the photograph had a rich and varied history. The North Western Hotel sign can be clearly seen, but the building had been the Rose and Punchbowl Hotel before the London, North Western Railway took it over. The building itself is a fine example of the architecture of a bygone age, with an eye-catching style and symmetry, not least the roof gables with their ornamental tops. The street scene below the windows of the hotel is rather mundane, although the link with the railways is maintained by the three-wheeled railway mechanical horse approaching in the distance. The Morris Minor coming up the street helps to set the scene in the 1950s.

A variety of shops and little businesses, along with some interesting architectural styles, would have greeted your eye as you progressed down Newland into Market Square in 1958. The shop with the Castrol sign on the far left had been the Goff & Lee cycle shop, but at this date belonged to Andre Baldet. Across Princess Street stood the old Temperance Hall Cinema, and its sign is clear to be seen on the attractive frontage overlooking Newland. A little further down the left-hand side of the street would have found you at the Popular Café, whilst just around the corner was the historic Welsh house. This was playing host to a garage and a school of motoring in 1958. A

splendid Austin Princess makes an appearance on the far right, whilst further down the street the CIU sign invites you to slake your thirst at the Century Club, an imposing Working Men's Club. The 'Chronicle & Echo' van is parked at the rear entrance of the newspaper offices. In the background across Market Square, Roses Fashion Centre, in Waterloo House, catches the eye. By 1972 this part of Newland had been swept away as part of the Grosvenor Centre development.

It may be going to work time or coming home time; either way it's a fairly busy time on Horseshoe Street sometime in the 1950s. The gaslamps put the picture in that decade, as do the vehicles on display. In some ways the brightest spots on the photograph are the billboards behind the cyclists. The advertisements illuminate what otherwise appears to be a rather grey day. Some of the products advertised have stood the test of time, and some familiar names are there. However, whatever happened to Tide, seemingly 'loved by women' and 'the greatest wash of all'? Booth's Gin was known at the 'Gentleman's gin', reputedly it was a favourite of both Queen Elizabeth II and the Queen Mother. Horseshoe Street had the wonderfully named Gasometer Public House on its right hand side, but the construction of the huge traffic junction in this area has now placed this scene in the nostalgia category.

Town and city centres are constantly under a process of change and this part of Northampton has been transformed since this photograph of Newland was taken, not many years after the Second World War ended. There is some degree of modernity in that a one-way system has been instituted, but otherwise this image belongs very much to the past. Nevertheless many residents of Northampton will remember the familiar landmarks of the 'Chronicle and Echo' offices and the Century Club up the left-hand side of the street. There is a line of very solid looking vehicles parked down the right-hand side of Newland, outside Dewhirsts and the Popular Café. Perhaps most interesting of all is the historic Welsh house at the bottom of Newland which, at this stage, accommodated a garage and a school of motoring. The inscription (to the right of the garage sign) is in Welsh and translates as, 'Without God Nothing. With God Enough.' The whole of this part of Newland was swept away in changes that created the Grosvenor Centre Shopping Mall in 1972.

A New Theatre enclosed by scaffolding, and on the verge of complete demolition, is the sad theme of this 1960 photograph. How could this living theatre have died? Perhaps it was the rise of the cinema. Film-going rose in popularity throughout the 1930s and peaked in the 40s and 50s. Many old music halls and variety theatres saw no other course of survival than to become cinemas themselves. The New Theatre had only a brief flirtation with films, between 1933 and 1934. Postwar audiences were sparse, in spite of the appearance of major entertainment figures such as John Gielgud, Claire Bloom, Arthur Askey and Jimmy Edwards. It was perhaps a desperate response to this that caused the management of the New Theatre to turn to strip shows in the 1950s. This had the effect of destroying the theatre's reputation for family entertainment. Strenuous attempts were made to save it but the last show in 1958. An attempt was made to preserve the four stone urns on the parapet, and the photograph shows Mr Lou Warwick, the acknowledged expert on the New Theatre, as proud possessor of one of them.

The view along Bridge Street give us a snapshot of life in 1950s Northampton. It was taken with the photographer's back to St John's RC Church. St John's Street is the cobbled thoroughfare to the right. We can see from the clock that it was 2.55pm when the photograph was taken. A group of men look at a motorcycle outside Coldham's, who was a long established motorcycle dealer. Business boomed as young men tried to impress their girlfriends with riding skills copied from Geoff Duke. Coldham's came to a dramatic end when the shop collapsed whilst building work was taking place next door. Fortunately, the incident happened at night and no one was hurt.

A bird's eye view from the high-rise flats in 'The Boroughs', the area of Spring Lane and Scarletwell Street, looks south-eastwards. The late 1950s and early 1960s saw redevelopment begin in earnest in the central areas of Northampton, and the block of flats from which this photograph was taken was the first of the highrise structures. The immediate foreground view shows that more were to follow. The foundations of former buildings are visible on the left and the dilapidated state of the properties to the right, along with the heavy wagon's presence, show that demolition is imminent. The historic market space of the Mayorhold, to the right, was soon to disappear. Keeping to this

side of the picture, the name of Nicholson Wool Merchant might be visible, arched over the door of the large warehouse. To the left of this, the white building is the King's Head public house. Clusters of buildings densely pack the middleground, interspersed with clumps of trees. At top left, the skyline is dominated by the spire of the Church of the Holy Sepulchre, whilst just right of centre may be seen the distant water tower of the Lotus shoe factory in Newland.

An elevated view looking east from Market Square finds Abington Street thronged with shoppers. Fashions and vehicles indicate the 1950s and the numbers of people about suggest a time of day when, only a few years later, the traffic would be nose-to-tail down the street. These were calmer times, however, as far as cars were concerned and freer movement was allowed after the bottleneck which had blighted the street had been demolished in 1946. The site on the corner of Dychurch Lane, to the right, had not yet been developed when this photograph was taken. Much of the interest in the picture lies on the right-hand side. Above Wiggins & Co Ltd is a round sign indicating the offices of Friends Provident and Century Insurance. This has a splendidly solid and old-fashioned ring about it, but it is the nostrils of the older readers which might quiver at the mention of Kingham's Grocers. This too was to be found in the block of buildings to the right and is best remembered for the aroma of roasting coffee which wafted out of it and along Abington Street.

There was no missing the offices of the Northampton Gaslight Company which used to stand on the corner of Abington Street and Wellington Street. That the building was actually constructed for the Gas Company, rather than built for some other purpose, is revealed by the fact that 'GAS' is literally carved there in stone. It was certainly an imposing, not to say overpowering edifice, and no doubt hundreds of people found their daily employment there. Another person who must have found plenty of work there is the window cleaner whose handcart and ladders are parked outside the spacious entrance. The number of windows to be cleaned suggests that it was a very worthwhile contract. The handcart has a touch of nostalgia about it, for window cleaners tend to be motorised today. Again, the white-coated delivery boy cycling up the street with his basket to the fore is a rare sight now, and the scenario has a 1950s look about it. The Gas Company's building has that very functional look of 1930s architecture. If that is the case it did not have too long a lifespan, for it was demolished in 1969 to make way for a Marks and Spencer store.

The H Samuel clock tells us that it is 11.18am in this 1950s shot of The Drapery from the top of Bridge Street, and this was one clock that just had to be right. The Drapery is impressively framed by the fine buildings of Boots and H Samuel to the left, and the imposing structure of the Westminster Bank to the right, complete with dome. The bus in the distance is of the old open-ended variety, which gave you a sporting chance of swinging onto the platform at the first corner if you had just missed it.

The wetness of the day does not seem to have deterred the shoppers as they throng Abington Street. In fact there seems to be an air of urgency about as three ladies cross the Wood Hill corner apparently oblivious of the vehicle bearing down on them. This in itself was an interesting one, an electric delivery van belonging to the bakery department of the Northampton Co-operative Society. Perhaps its quietness and appearance made it seem less menacing than the ordinary bread van. This shot of the 1950s captured a side of Abington Street with a variety of nice architecture and some interesting names. The Fifty Shilling Tailors - how evocative of another age that one shop name is! It is not just the different currency, but the price itself. How much can you buy in the way of clothing for £2.50 now? Readers of a certain vintage might remember what you could buy for it then at The Fifty Shilling Tailors. It is possible that the photograph was taken in the New Year, for Burtons is offering a 'Half Price Sale'. These tended to be in the New Year, unlike now when Sales seem to go on the year round.

Many Northampton people may still remember the old junction of the Harborough and Welford Roads before the road pattern was changed in the early 1960s. Although there are some fairly 'antique' vehicles in the garage forecourt to the right, the presence of a Morris Minor heading towards the town centre probably places this picture in the 1950s. Accustomed as we are to large, very readable green signs at major junctions, the little old black and white signs seem piffling in comparison, easily missed at night or in poor visibility. To the right, the Welford Road takes motorists to Leicester, whilst the Harborough Road goes straight on into Northampton town centre, and points beyond. The name 'Cleveland' should evoke some memories for those who were motorists in this era, along with the distinctively shaped petrol pump tops. No such thing as self-service pumps in those days. You were likely to be served by somebody wiping their hands on an oily rag who would have given you a very funny look if you had asked for crisps and chocolates as well! It was a nice touch to thank customers in such a prominent way, but the garage was to disappear in the changes to come.

If London buses tend to travel in threes, then Northampton buses progress in convoys of nine or ten, might be the first impression given by this picture. In fact the queue of buses in Market Square was part of a Holidays at Home promotion by the Corporation Transport Department in the immediate post-war years. People had not been encouraged to travel during the Second World War. Petrol was in short supply and economy was the order of the day. Things did not improve greatly even when the war was over and hence the Holidays at Home campaign. During Northampton's annual summer shoe holiday fortnight, those who still could not get away could at least enjoy entertainments put on by the Corporation. One of the diversions was a bus tour of the suburbs which were in the process of being developed after 1945. In the background the distinctive white facade of Burtons can be seen behind the buses, with Waterloo House to the far right.

MEMORIES OF NORTHAMPTON

The 1960s ushered in the age of the high-rise flats. It seemed a neat enough solution at the time to the problem of housing people relatively cheaply in the face of the spiralling costs of buying building land. Go upwards - New York fashion. The photograph shows the first of the Northampton high-rise flats being erected in The Boroughs, the area of Spring Lane and Scarletwell Street. More were to follow, and even the Mayorhold, an ancient market space in the foreground, was soon to disappear. Nobody at the time was able to forecast the social problems of high-rise living, or how quickly the planners dreams of the 60s would become discredited. To the right of the picture, Grafton Street can be traced upwards and then Spencer Bridge, crossing the railway tracks. If high-rise flats spoke of the future, the railway marshalling yards in the background spoke of the past. The hundreds of goods wagons show how much freight was still carried by British Rail even in the 1960s. This was to go into sad decline with the rise of motorways and the huge expansion of freight transport by road, but who can deny that here too progress has brought its own problems?

The corner with Mercer's Row and the Drapery is shown in the mid 1920s just before Knight's and Son, on the left, had their premises knocked down. They were to make way for a complete remodelling of this site. A new building, housing the Westminster Bank, was to appear on the site. The cobbles are still in place today, but the tram en route to St James would be travelling in the wrong direction today, as traffic flow is one way along Mercer's Row towards Abington Street. The Grade I listed All Saints' Church is a 1680 replacement of medieval parish church. The men lounging on the wall of the church remind us that this was a period of economic downturn and that many were unable to find work.

Looking up Abington Street from Mercers Row, Wood Hill is to the right and Market Square away to the left. Henry Price established his Fifty Shilling Tailors outlets, selling cheap, but acceptable, clothing. His shop in Northampton stood on the corner known to old Northamptonians as Doffman's Corner. It was named after the firm of tailors that had been on the site before Henry Price came to town. It is one of the town's oldest buildings. Burton's, on the opposite corner from the Fifty Shilling shop, was a more upmarket competitor. The Belisha beacons around Doffman's Corner were a necessary indication showing pedestrians where to cross the road in some safety. Abington Street Northampton's main shopping street and has since been pedestrianised.

Royal visits to Northampton

A fabulous image from the Royal visit in 1932 of the Duke and Duchess of York, later to become King George VI and Queen Elizabeth the Queen Mother. They were in Northampton to open the new College of Technology, Avenue Campus, and visit the John Greenwood Shipman Convalescent Home. Huge crowds had gathered along the streets to get a view of the royal couple on their journey from the now disused Blisworth Station. In the picture, we can see them alighting from the royal car outside the County Hall in George Row.

In February 1942, a small unit of the United States Army Air Force (USAAF) was set up in High Wycombe. The wing of the 1st Air Division covered Northamptonshire and Cambridgeshire. The Americans used a number of local airfields that included RAF Grafton Underwood, designated USAAF 106 and RAF Kettering (Harrington), or USAAF 179, that was used later on in the war. Two years later, the Eighth Air Force had grown to become the biggest military air fleet ever seen. In 1946, Queen Elizabeth, wife of George VI, and her daughter, Princess Elizabeth, called at an American base during their visit to the county. This helped illustrate the debt that we owed to our allies from across the Atlantic and, in particular, to those who could never return to their homeland.

In the second image from the 1932 royal visit, the Duchess appears to be particularly relaxed in the photographs, whilst members of the official party seem rather more stiff and formal. The Duchess was seen to be radiating the charm for which she was to become famous. The official party included the Mayor and Mayoress, Councillor and Mrs P F Hanafy, Colonel John Brown and John Williamson, the Chief Constable.

Princess Elizabeth, with Earl Spencer just to the rear, proceeds down an aisle of nurses on her departure from Northampton General Hospital. July 30th 1946 was a 'red letter' day for the town, marking as it did Princess Elizabeth's first official visit. A spot of royal pageantry and colour was an ideal morale booster in these grim post-war years, with rationing and shortages still blighting the country. The visit, however, had a definite purpose. In 1944 the hospital war appeal for £250,000 had been launched, with each town and village in the area allotted a target. The Princess was visiting the hospital to award souvenir cards to the delegates of 103 places which had exceeded their targets. Huge, enthusiastic crowds greeted the royal car as it made its way from the borough boundary to the General Hospital. Flag-waving schoolchildren cheered at the tops of their voices, and the corner of Cheyne Walk and St Giles Street found people perched on window sills and even roofs. Before touring the hospital, Princess Elizabeth presented the token cards. Each one outlined the nature of the award, accompanied by the phrase, 'Sweet mercy is nobility's true badge'.

On leaving the nurses' home at the General Hospital, the Princess made the short walk to the childrens' ward and the Barratt Maternity Home. Having left the formality of the presentation behind, it was during this part of the visit that the happiest and most touching scenes of the day were enacted. The Princess met children whose ages ranged from five days to nine years, and children are nothing if not spontaneous. Outside the children's ward, in the warm sunshine, she chatted with 14 children surrounded by their toys. She seemed delighted by their responses, not least by the fact that two of them slept soundly, blissfully unaware of the royal presence. She was obviously moved, however, by the plight of some of the sick children. Princess Elizabeth then went on to mingle with the mothers and expectant mothers in the Maternity Home. The latter was presented to Northampton by Mr W Barratt, the prominent shoe manufacturer. Hence, 'to walk the Barratt way' in Northampton, means to be pregnant. It is doubtful if anyone informed the Princess of this! The photograph shows her inspecting an ATS guard of honour on her departure. The Princess herself had served with the ATS during the war.

At Leisure

No stern and straight-faced pose for the camera as is so often seen in old photographs. These young ladies offer only friendly smiles as they perambulate along Paradise Walk in 1937. The picture was taken from the bottom of Cheyne Walk, looking towards Bedford Road, and is evocative in so many ways. The railings on the right enclosed land that was then known as Cow Meadow and there may be some senior citizens who remember Frisian cows grazing there. It is, of course now known as Becket's Park. The railings have been removed and the asphalt path replaced by grass. The cooling tower to the right belonged to the Hardingstone Junction Power Station, and was later joined by two others. They have all since been demolished. But back to the young ladies. Paradise Walk was clearly a lovely place to stroll and chat whilst taking baby on an outing, and possibly these were nannies. There is just a suggestion, however, that these are not young ladies, but young girls pushing dolls prams.

There is no mistaking Tom Walls, the dapper little gentleman in the middle of the front row. A famous stage and screen star of the 1930s, he is pictured here with the staff of the Exchange Cinema. Tom was born at Byron Street in Northampton and he first achieved fame in the Aldwych farces with Robertson Hare. His great passion other than acting was horses, and he later went to live at the nearby village of Chapel Brampton, from which he was more easily able to follow his beloved Pytchley Hunt. As a great horseracing enthusiast, he achieved a lifetime ambition when his horse, 'April V', won the Epsom Derby in 1932. Tom's appearance at the Exchange Cinema was on the occasion of the premiere of one of his films, 'The Blarney Stone'. The Exchange had opened in 1920 and was the town's most palatial cinema. The bow-tied manager, 'Pat' Thornton, stands on the right. The advertisement for Boris Karloff, in 'The Old Dark House', is enough to send shivers down the spine of older readers.

The simple fun and pleasure of drinking at a public fountain seems now to belong to a far-off age. Indeed the dress of the children seems to put this scene back into the 1930s or 1940s, although this type of drinking fountain still had a good few years to run yet. What is most striking about the big boy are his 'long short' trousers and his sturdy boots. But if you can't wear boots in Northampton, then where can you wear them? He is helping with the tap, and those who experienced it will remember the hexagonal shape which gave you enough grip to abruptly turn the fountain of water up. Then the little bubble of water became a jet, and it might be suspected that the little boy is about to feel this up his nose. Of course, for the little girl, the achievement will be for her to get her lips to the water at all. This particular fountain was located in Abington Park, near the wall between the bowling green and the thatched farm outbuilding. They were originally installed as a service to the community, but modern health requirements have seen the fountains banished from our parks forever.

A ny moment now there will be a large splash, and probably an excited scream, as the first of the figures on the platform careers down the water chute. This happy summer scene was captured in 1956 at Overstone Solarium, a pleasure park on the outskirts of town. Britain does not have the ideal climate for open-air swimming pools, but on the right day it can be an exhilarating experience to swim or just splash about - all in the glorious fresh air. On the other hand, you can choose just to laze around and watch. The line of spectators behind the roof ridge have certainly got a 'bird's eye view'. Whether idly spectating or taking to the water, people are relaxing and enjoying themselves. Swimming has grown in popularity since the growth of municipal baths in the nineteenth century. These were designed partly for recreation, and partly to deter people from swimming in rivers, canals and dams, with all the attendant risks to health and safety. The pool at Overstone Solarium was a very fine one, but its future fate can be glimpsed at top right. The pleasure park became a caravan site, with the pool sliced in half to leave a small paddling pool.

Little Tony Forward's career was mapped out almost from the start and here he is at the tender age of four, learning to cope with the media. Tony, a Northampton boy, was the son of Alan Forward (pictured on the left) who was a successful grass track racer. Tony became the mascot of the Brandon Bees speedway team, and he led them around on their parade laps. This is where it might have ended, for child mascots in all sports tend to disappear into their different walks of life at a later stage. However, motor-cycle racing was in Tony's blood, and he went on to ride the Continental circuit as a professional speedway and grass track racer with great success. Speedway racing has had bouts of great popularity since the war and it can certainly provide an exciting spectacle. A first time visitor is usually amazed by the sheer noise as the bikes open up and jostle for position on the first bend, or is intrigued by that distinctive smell of high octane fuel hanging in the air. Tony became 'hooked' by the thrills and spills, and from watching his heroes he went on to become a big name himself.

A sight to inspire terror in the stoutest defence as a close formation of footballing fillies approaches, using not just one ball but two! Girls' football teams are quite common today, but it was once a novelty to see the 'fairer sex' in soccer kit. These were, in fact, chorus girls from the New Theatre who had come to the County Ground and donned the colours of the 'Cobblers' for a publicity shot. The eye-catching and unusual picture then appeared in the 'Chronicle and Echo' as an inducement to Northamptonians to 'Come to the Show,' for indeed that was what the show was called. The New Theatre closed its doors for ever in 1958 and the photograph seems to date from the earlier part of that decade. The baggy shorts and collared shirts point to that time, along with leather footballs that turned to 'puddings' in wet weather. It would be interesting to know if this publicity stunt had any success, for overall the New Theatre went into steady decline in the post-war years. More intriguingly, did the players of Northampton Town ever appear as 'chorus girls' at the New Theatre in order to boost gates?

There was little protection for these bathers at Midsummer Meadow baths in the summer of 1966. Hardly anyone bothered with head covering. On this day some 3,000 had come through the turnstiles by teatime. The pool was legendary for its freezing waters, but on this day they frolicked in the warm water out in the open air. Midsummer Meadow outdoor swimming pool or public baths had opened in 1908 and the heating came from the nearby generating station. After the war, during the summer school holidays most children from the town would make their way to Midsummer Meadow to go swimming or paddling. it was a good cheap day out and moms could sit on the grass and watch everyone in the water or talk to other mothers sitting near by. If all went well, we might get a treat on the way home like a bag of marmite crisps and a bottle of fizzy pop. The pool was demolished in 1983.

Scenes of unrestrained joy greet the photographer in the Northampton dressing room as an historic occasion is celebrated. By securing a 1-1 draw at home with Portsmouth, in front of an ecstatic crowd of 20,660, the 'Cobblers' had attained First Division status for the first time in their history. Despite the humble beer crate on the table, it's the champagne corks that are popping. Devoted football fans watch their little dramas played out on the pitch and soon come to accept that this week's joy could be next week's despair. Followers of the 'Cobblers,' however, between 1958 and 1970 saw drama on an epic scale, and the ultimate feeling may well have been one of disbelief. Between 1958 and 1965 Northampton Football Club made an extraordinary surge through four divisions to find itself playing alongside football's elite. By August 1965, under skipper Theo Foley, the 'Cobblers' were kicking off against Everton in their first ever top division match. Unfortunately the club was relegated at the end of that season, and again the following season. By 1970 the 'Cobblers' were back in the Fourth Division. The only possible consolation to travelling fans was that it gave them the chance to visit every Football League ground in the country!

It's 1932 and one of the hottest heat-waves for years. The little boy is dressed for the occasion in the height of swimsuit fashion, but he has sensibly kept his footwear on. No doubt the road was burning hot under his feet. Protection against the sun was pretty rudimentary is those far-off days. Nobody had even heard of thinning ozone layers and dangerous ultra-violet rays. As for high factor sun cream ... well, a dab of calamine lotion if you were lucky, usually after the damage had been done! It's not clear what the policeman is doing. He may be stopping the traffic (which seems to be non-existent); or he may be sending the lad home to put something respectable on; or he may be pointing the way to the nearest paddling pool. One thing is for certain, he will have to sweat it out in his blue serge uniform. No walking about in shirt sleeves for bobbies in those days! Long, hot summers are the stuff of childhood memories, along with sticky fly papers hanging from the ceiling if you go back far enough. But let's not forget that the year of the drought was only back in 1995.

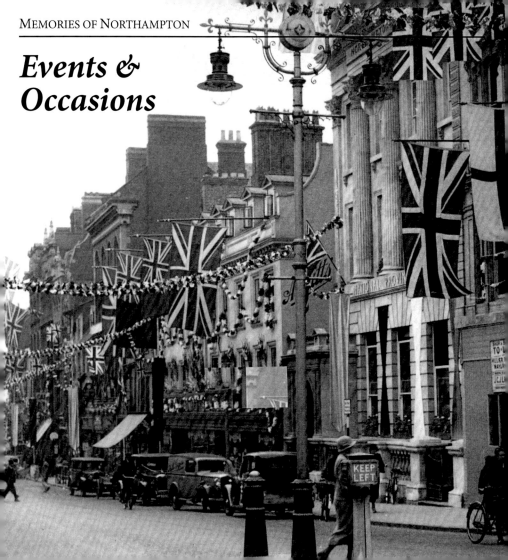

Events & Occasions

Left: May 12th 1937 marked the Coronation of King George VI and Queen Elizabeth. In common with the rest of the country, Northampton celebrated the occasion with rejoicing and patriotic fervour. People were glad of a joyous royal event which might relieve the general gloom of national and international affairs at that time. Northampton streets were lavishly decorated for the great day and this photograph left shows The Drapery. Shops and public buildings are hung with giant flags, and streamers crisscross the street.

Above: Tremendous efforts were made to bring colour and pageantry into the streets of Northampton in May 1937, and the local council did a fine job in having several triumphal arches erected in the town centre. This wonderful effort was to be found on Abington Street. It manages to combine a patriotic and loyal message with a neat reference to Northampton's traditional involvement in leather and shoes. More decorations are visible further along the street and even the barrels housing the temporary erecting posts have been given fancy wrappings. The rather impressive building housing the Northampton Town and County Building Society, far right, is plentifully adorned with streamers, emblems and flags.

The newly constructed All Saints Parish Hall, on Horseshoe Street is absolutely packed for a Coronation celebration tea on May 12th 1937. There seems to be not an inch to spare as the guests pause a moment for the photographer before falling on the sandwiches, buns and fizzy drinks. It is an occasion that is clearly meant for children in the main, although not entirely so. Some patriotic hats are on display and from the clothing worn by some of the children, there is just a suggestion that a fancy dress parade has been incorporated into the day's events. At the rear of the hall, distinguished visitors look on benignly and no doubt they will be nibbling at a little something themselves. It is interesting to speculate what state those beautifully clean tablecloths were in by the end of the afternoon. The line of helpers standing along the left-hand wall, many of them in 'pinnies', had no doubt slaved for hours to prepare this feast. And, even on Coronation Day, somebody has to do the washing up. Imagine what that would amount to in an age where there were no such things as disposable plastic plates and cups!

Plenty of smiles for the camera outside All Saints Parish Hall on that Coronation Day of over 60 years ago. Most of these youngsters will now be senior citizens, but there might still be one or two copies of this photograph tucked away in albums somewhere, a treasured memory. Keen-eyed readers might be able to identify some of the faces here in the other photograph concerning All Saints. Plenty of imagination has gone into the fancy dress, with probably the most lightweight jockey of all time on the front row. The patriotically decorated bike too deserves to have won a prize. Scenes like this were repeated across Northampton as scores of streets and roads hung up their decorations and celebrated the Coronation. Games, sports, teas, music, dancing, motor bus tours of the town centre decorations - these were the recurrent themes. There were, however, more unusual aspects. On St David's Road there was an 'ankle competition'. All the children of Vicarage Lane, Kingsthorpe, had a TSB account opened for them. Younger children on Dallington Road received a Coronation mug, filled with chocolates, whilst older boys received an engraved pocket knife, and girls an inscribed compact. Most mysterious of all, Wantage Road held a 'smoking competition!'

MEMORIES OF NORTHAMPTON

This view of St Giles Street on Coronation Day 1937 just takes in the corner of the Town Hall, on the left, showing to good effect some of the fine carvings on this building. To the right, the substantial and solid edifice of the Prudential Building houses its own offices and the premises of Montagu Jeffrey underneath. Once again streamers and flags are to the fore as the street prepares itself for the events of the day ahead. Perhaps the policeman cycling his way up the street in the distance was on his way to his duty point for the Grand Parade. The latter was one of the major events of Northampton's celebrations of May 12th and it involved 50 decorated lorries in a procession that was nearly one mile long. It was led by the Syncopated Players' Band, closely followed by the Shoe Trade Queen, Miss Winifred Bull, surrounded by Union Jacks. The lorries that followed each carried a tableau depicting an episode in the history of Northampton, or a depiction of the town's life and work. All this was staged by Northampton schoolchildren who had rehearsed and worked for weeks in preparation for the event.

The shadows across Bridge Street give an indication that Coronation Day 1937 turned out to be a sunny one. No doubt the sunshine enhanced the patriotic colours on the streamers and flags. A BSA motorbike with delivery sidecar is parked in a rough and ready fashion at the right-hand side of the street. Lee's tobacconists, on the far right, proudly advertises its 'Superb Abdullah Cigarettes', whilst lower down the sign for 'Foyles 2d Library' gives some idea of the humble beginnings of this now large organisation. The man leaning on the belisha beacon seems to have no intention of crossing the road. Many shots of the 1930s feature working men in regulation flathats and mufflers in a 'nothing to do, nowhere to go' pose. Perhaps this one is simply staking his claim early for a good view of the Grand Parade. In which case he will have been treated to dozens of tableaux including, 'Homage to Learning' by the girls of Northampton School, clad in Greek robes; the 'Trial of Thomas a Becket at Northampton Castle,' by Spencer School; or even, the 'English Gypsies Salute Their King' by the Roadmender Boys' Club.

MEMORIES OF NORTHAMPTON

Carnival time was popular with everyone. In 1937 thousands lined the streets to watch the parade of floats making their way up Gold Street into George Row. It came as a welcome distraction from the worrying news from Europe. The storm clouds of war were gathering. In the processions were the contraptions that had been gaily decked with garlands and bunting to set off the festive scene. Later there would be games and sports in the parks. The fairground would be alive with the noise of happy folk enjoying the dodgems, coconut shies and merry go rounds. In the meantime the crowd thrilled at the ingenuity of the float designers. The main one pictured was called 'Showboat'. It was an entry by the Rushden shoe company of John White Ltd. Not surprisingly, it won the championship cup. Northampton's carnival had a long history. It began in 1890 as a cycle parade. At the time there were 12 cycling clubs in the town. The carnival raised funds for the General Hospital.

Memories of Northampton

There was something definitely afoot on the wide spaces of Abington Street in June 1953. A fairly quiet time of day has been chosen for putting the final touches to the decorations, or perhaps it was even the morning of the great day itself - June 2nd 1953. A feeling of barely suppressed excitement lay beneath the calm for this day was a landmark, the Coronation of Queen Elizabeth II, the dawn of the new Elizabethan Age. It was time at last to shake off the drab years of post-war austerity. The centre of Northampton became a sea of colour - mainly red, white and blue -as shops and public buildings were festooned with flags, emblems, bunting and streamers. Huge banners and emblematic crowns were the theme of Abington Street, although a massive Union Jack has been unfurled from the roof of the rather splendid looking Notre Dame Convent and School, to the right. Elsewhere in the town centre the story was much the same as the people of Northampton set out to show that, in terms of patriotism, they were second to none.

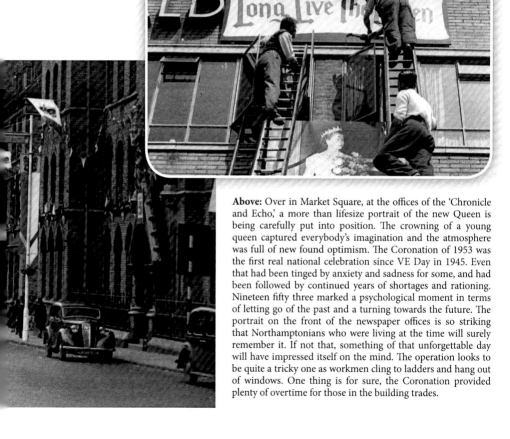

Above: Over in Market Square, at the offices of the 'Chronicle and Echo,' a more than lifesize portrait of the new Queen is being carefully put into position. The crowning of a young queen captured everybody's imagination and the atmosphere was full of new found optimism. The Coronation of 1953 was the first real national celebration since VE Day in 1945. Even that had been tinged by anxiety and sadness for some, and had been followed by continued years of shortages and rationing. Nineteen fifty three marked a psychological moment in terms of letting go of the past and a turning towards the future. The portrait on the front of the newspaper offices is so striking that Northamptonians who were living at the time will surely remember it. If not that, something of that unforgettable day will have impressed itself on the mind. The operation looks to be quite a tricky one as workmen cling to ladders and hang out of windows. One thing is for sure, the Coronation provided plenty of overtime for those in the building trades.

A wonderful splash of colour must have greeted the photographer's eye as he captured this scene in the closing room of J Sears & Co, shoe manufacturers. Wherever the people of Northampton came together to work - shops, mills, schools, hospitals - imaginative minds and busy hands produced decorations that were fit for a new monarch and a new era. The ladies at Sears (and a few men) are in party mood judging by their cheerful faces and the amount of 'liquid refreshment' on the go. They earned their break too considering the amount of effort that must have gone into the superb decorations. As they were hanging the streamers they may well have been humming along to the big 'hit' melody of the time, 'Elizabethan Serenade.' Many may remember that evocative piece of music, which seemed to be on the radio every two minutes. It is difficult to imagine that those sewing machines ever really got cracking again that day, or that those piles of leather got much smaller!

A travelling circus advertised its presence in the town with a parade of stiltwalkers, clowns, tumblers, jugglers and a family of elephants. One trader in Market Square was less than happy to see Nellie and her companions as they raided his wares, consuming a barrow load of produce that he could ill afford to lose. The buildings in the background include one used by Church's China and Glass Company. It was set up by Thomas Church in 1858 when he took over premises in Devizes. With the assistance of son Wesley, the firm came to Northampton in the early 1870s. Wesley married Sarah Spencer, a shoemaker's daughter, and they set up both shop and home in Parade House, a former hotel on the north side of Market Square. Successive generations of the family ran the business until the founder's great grandson, Vivian, took over the other side of the front of the Arcade as well in the 1960s. A move was made to Welsh House on the square in 1975.

The workman sums up his options as he stands, fairly securely, on the roof above the entrance to the ABC Cinema. He almost appears to be consulting the portrait of Prince Philip as to where to place the roundels of the young children, Charles and Anne. The Queen's family were not forgotten in the 1953 Coronation celebrations, for this was part of the appeal, a young couple with a young family. People could identify with this. Youth was increasingly to come to the fore in the 1950s and the launching of a new magazine, 'The Young Elizabethan,' seemed to capture the mood of it all. Once the portraits were erected, passers-by enjoyed a good view from the street below, and an even better one from the top deck of a bus, of a happy family scene.

When the much awaited day of June 2nd 1953 at last arrived, the British weather naturally rose to the occasion. It was generally dull and cold, with squally bursts of rain. Nevertheless the people of Northampton were determined to enjoy themselves and the weather did not prevent an eruption of street parties which had been planned for months. The photographer has caught an absolute sea of colour along Gladstone Terrace in a scene that was so typical of the day. Most of the celebrations took place in the afternoon as everyone wanted to watch the Coronation ceremony on television around midday. In 1953, of course, televisions were quite a rarity and there was a good deal of communal viewing of televisions set up in school and church halls. The screens were small; the images were black-and-white and of poor quality; but anyone who watched that day will not have forgotten the experience. Then it was off to the street parties! The children of Gladstone Terrace are obviously enjoying themselves. There are plenty of caps and short pants in evidence, for there was no pressure for children to look 'cool'.

The importance of the occasion cannot be lost on these children of Stimpson Avenue School as they collect their Coronation souvenirs in June 1953. Some trouble has been gone to in the erecting of a little dais and in the draping of Union Jacks to form a patriotic backcloth. The sight of that highly polished chair on the dais might evoke an instant recollection of school days to some. That style of teacher's chair, once so common in schools, is quite a rarity in the classroom now. The ceremony of the occasion is an indication of just how loyal the country was to the institution of monarchy in 1953. There was no hint of modern day cynicism in ordinary people's attitudes towards the Crown. It would be surprising if these children had not sung the National Anthem at the end of the presentation, for it was played as a matter of course at all public performances. Not only this, people invariably stood up respectfully. Most probably there was a Coronation mug in the box that the little girl is clutching so earnestly. How many readers got one? How many have still got it?

What a splendid effort was made by the residents of Manor Road, Kingsthorpe, in their fancy-dress parade to celebrate the 1953 Coronation. The little jockey at the front, to the right, is dressed in honour of the great horseracing hero of the day, Gordon Richards. A jockey of a different kind can be seen on the left as the little sheriff 'rides into the sunset' on his wooden horse. Adults and children alike have entered into the spirit of it all. Similar scenes were enacted in countless Northampton streets on that memorable day. Huge quantities of ice-cream and jelly were consumed; souvenir presents were distributed; there were games, races, competitions and treasure hunts. Gwyn Hughes, a wing-half for the 'Cobblers' opened the festivities at Danefield Road, whilst at Gloucester Street Close they were celebrating the winning of the best-decorated street competition. The rain had its way later in the day when the evening fireworks display and decorated boat procession at Becket's Park had to be postponed. Nevertheless the local firemen did not allow the weather to disrupt their display of water jets illuminated by coloured spotlights.

MEMORIES OF NORTHAMPTON

The Second World War disturbed all sorts of things, in this case the celebrations for the four hundredth anniversary of the founding of Northampton Town and County Grammar School. The school having been founded by Thomas Chipsey in 1541, this important commemoration should have taken place in 1941, but the war put paid to that. Instead it was held in 1947, and the photograph shows Air Chief Marshal Sir Philip Joubert unveiling a plaque over the main entrance to mark the occasion. The school, now the Northampton School for Boys, had interesting origins. It was established in 1541 in what had been St Gregory's Church. This old church had contained a shrine known as the 'rood in the wall.' Here, long ago, a vision of an angel had appeared and declared Northampton to be the centre of England. Whether this had any influence on generations of Geography teachers at the school is not known. The ceremony pictured gives every appearance of having been a splendid occasion. The link with the air-force is clear from the lines of smart air cadets standing at ease. Proud parents look on, and the shorts and pumps on display seem to indicate that a Sports Day will follow.

The strains of Roll Out the Barrel, hugely popular with the troops during World War Two, will be forever associated with the vivacious Bertha Willmott, pictured here with her husband, Reg Seymour. Bertha's roots were in London. She was born in East Ham, in 1895, and her singing talent was encouraged by the nuns at the convent school she attended. Having begun her stage career in 1912 as Little Mollie, she reverted to her own name in 1914. Radio was to become Bertha's forte and she began to make a name for herself in such programmes as Henry Hall's Guest Night. Northampton first saw this rising star in 1932 when she appeared at the New Theatre in Ridgeway Parade with Ben Warris (although she had appeared earlier in her career as a singer at Rushden Working Men's Club for a fee of £1 15 shillings!). Something about Northampton and its people appealed to Bertha, for in 1938 she and Reg took over the Spinney Hill Hotel. Bertha's career reached its peak during the war when, as part of ENSA, she helped to entertain troops on the radio programme Your Cup of Tea. In her later years she was involved in the campaign to try and save the New Theatre. Her death came in 1978.

Something was certainly afoot in Market Square on the morning of July 9th 1965, and the sight of so many uniforms might suggest a crisis. However, the army and police were not there to quell civil disorder in the streets of Northampton. Further examination of the photograph reveals bandsmen, nurses and boy scouts. All these uniformed groups had been brought in by bus and van to play their part in what was to be a very happy occasion - the visit of Queen Elizabeth II and the Duke of Edinburgh to the town. The maroon Rolls Royce crossed the borough boundary at Weston Favell for the Queen's first visit to Northampton as a reigning monarch. Hundreds of flag-waving and cheering children made sure that she received a very special welcome. The crowds were extremely dense towards the town centre, some people having gained vantage points at top floor windows, or even on roof tops. 'Doesn't she look lovely,' was the cry as the Queen, in a lemon outfit, stepped out of the Rolls Royce at the Guildhall. Here the royal couple were entertained to lunch by the Mayor and Mayoress, Councillor and Mrs Don Wilson, before proceeding on their way, once more to great displays of enthusiasm.

Below: Flames shoot through the roof and a huge pall of smoke fills the sky. This dramatic scene was captured some 40 years ago, in September 1959, as the Wright Bros warehouse on the Mounts was consumed by one of the fiercest fires seen in Northampton for many years. The firemen struggled desperately, but the smoke does not quite obscure the notice towards the top of the warehouse indicating that huge stocks of furniture were housed within. Hence the fierceness of the blaze. To make matters worse, the firm next door, Edward C Cook, was a supplier of chemicals for leather, amongst other things. The tremendous heat caused the brickwork of St Mary's RC School, to the right, to flake and crumble.

Right: It looks as if the organisers managed to get a fine day for the Carnival Parade of 1955. These are always tremendously popular with young and old alike and an enthusiastic crowd lines the streets. As the Carnival Queen passes the Town Hall she is the focus of attention, but no doubt onlookers were appreciative of the floats that would be following on, not least the amount of work that always goes into them. A prize view has been gained by the people at the windows above the Corner House. The Carnival Queen and her retinue sit in state before a historical backdrop, with the town motto above - 'Castello Fortior Concordia'. Following on is a 'miniature' queen in a tiny float which seems to be one mass of flowers.

Left: We are a good ten years on from the end of the Cold War between the USA and the USSR, but from the late 1940s people lived with it as an everyday reality. Britain's own nuclear weapons, and the presence of American bases in our country, put Britain in the front line of any potential conflict. Most people accepted this as a fact of life, but the Campaign for Nuclear Disarmament (CND) vigorously opposed all nuclear weapons. 'Ban the Bomb' was the famous chant and equally famous was its logo. The first of the local CND protests took place at Wood Hill in 1962 and the tactics adopted were to become the hallmark of the movement - the 'sit down' protest. The policeman on the right is trying to talk the girl into moving, but no doubt she too will soon have to be dragged away to the Black Maria. Some of the customers of the Black Boy Hotel have bagged a grandstand view and the bus passengers are bemused by it all.

Right: Shoppers could have been excused for blinking twice at the surprising scene which greeted them in a town centre shop window sometime in 1967. After all, it is not too often that a bikini clad beauty takes a bath in public. This is what local girl and professional model, Jackie Mills, was promoting. Of course this was the 'swinging sixties', which was arguably the most socially transforming decade of the century. The mini-skirt, the 'pill', the Beatles, LSD - it all seemed light years away from the restrictive 1950s.

Left: Is it never going to start? This seems to be the thought written across the face of the young girl in the middle of the front row as this crowd of youngsters awaits the Punch and Judy show. The scene is the Abington Park Show in the early 1950s, and the limits of the fun you can get from swinging on a rope barrier look as if they have just about been reached. Never mind - no doubt the doleful expressions turned to delight as soon as Mr Punch squawked into action. The spacious Abington Park, with its boating lakes and pleasant walks, was once the private estate of Lady Wantage. In 1897, on the occasion of Queen Victoria's Diamond Jubilee, she presented the park to the town and retired to Overstone. Since then, it has provided the opportunity for fresh air and relaxation 'on the doorstep' for thousands of Northamptonians. During the Second World War, Abington Park became the venue for some of the 'Holidays at Home' entertainments. These were laid on by the local council during the summer holiday weeks because wartime travel restrictions and petrol shortages made getting away so difficult. After the war these annual events gradually evolved into the 'Town Show.'

Right: It's a happy looking rehearsal, although everybody seems to be doing pretty much their own thing'. The most instantly recognisable figure is Des O'Connor, and not far behind in this respect is Jim Dale, next but one to Des. Both these showbiz celebrities have local connections. Des was an evacuee who spent most of his early years in Northampton, whilst Jim hails from nearby Rothwell. Des was a redcoat at a holiday camp at which he won a national talent contest. To celebrate, he appeared at a show at the ABC Cinema, along with Jim Dale and others. The photograph has captured a cheerful moment during rehearsals for the show, which hairstyles and fashions would suggest was in the late 60s. The girl on the right is singing along with Des, whilst the others are simply enjoying the joke, although the girl to left of Des seems to be suffering from 'rehearsal fright'. Des went on to have a hugely successful career as a comedian and singer; more lately as a chat show host. His appearance has remained remarkably unaltered over the years. Jim Dale first made his mark as a 'pop' singer, but he is perhaps better known now for his comedy appearances in 'Carry On ...' films.

MEMORIES OF NORTHAMPTON

The day dawned bright and sunny for the coronation of King George VI. It was not the weather that was important. For the British the occasion was everything. In 1937 it was especially significant. The country had undergone the turmoil of the abdication crisis. King George's elder brother had refused to end his relationship with the American socialite Wallis Simpson. People were determined to show their support for the monarchy. This scene, looking north along the Drapery from All Saints Church, was repeated up and down the land. The Drapery is the name given to this entire street. To be accurate it should only apply to the left hand side. The opposite side is the Glovery, but the term is no longer in use. The names illustrate the trades that flourished here in earlier times. Mercers' Row is to the right of the imposing Westminster Bank building. Philadelphus Jeyes' pharmacy is one of the shops on the west side of the Drapery. It is the name behind Jeyes Fluid.

These folk living on Gloucester Crescent lived within a stone's throw of Delapre Park, across the other side of London Road. The land for the municipal park came from 586 acres purchased from the Bouverie estate. From 1957 Delapre Abbey housed the Northamptonshire Records Office. But dry and dusty records were of no interest to these little cherubs. Squinting into the sun, they posed for the camera in a variety of fancy dress costumes. Mums had been busy, treadling away to stitch and sew some grand outfits. Pirates crossed swords with guardsmen and majorettes vied with shepherdesses. The very smart young man at the front gives us a clue to the nature of the occasion, with his Union Jack shirt under his jacket. This was a fancy-dress parade to celebrate the 1953 Coronation of Queen Elizabeth II. After the photograph the children paraded before the street party judges. What a thankless task they had!

Linking St Giles Street and Hazelwood Road, near the old St Giles's Church building, is probably where this photograph was taken in June 1953. As the Queen made her way to Westminster Abbey for the Coronation ceremony, her subjects came onto the streets to join in the celebrations. There were processions and street parties, the like of which had not been seen since the end of the war. The day dawned damp and unseasonably cold. Wrapped up in warm coats, the children paraded in their fancy hats and wished Her Majesty well. Red, white and blue were everywhere and lads were happy to exchange their school caps for homemade patriotic ones. Despite the chilly conditions little boys and girls generally bared their knees to the elements in those days.

On the Move

Traffic jams come in all shapes and sizes, but a cyclist always has a chance of sneaking through somehow. For many years the level crossing at Cotton End provided an unwelcome obstacle for those travelling between the town centre and Far Cotton. Those precious few minutes could be vital, especially for those needing to clock in at work on time. This 1950s shot shows an option that was not open to the motorists. Of course it could be a toss up as to whether it was actually worthwhile to hoist your bike on your shoulder and use the footbridge, or whether the gates might open just as you reached the top of the steps, but the grin on the face of one of the cyclists seems to indicate that he knows something that the others don't! There are a good few fashion pointers to suggest that this might be the early 1950s, not least the cycle clips to hold in the baggy trousers of that time. It was either that or tucking your trousers into your socks to avoid that oily chain. Cycling gear is much more streamlined today, but the problems of weaving a way through dense urban traffic have much increased.

Along line of coaches belonging to local firm Wesley's stretches its way along the side of Market Square almost to Burtons in the background. This scene was captured on a hot summer's day in the 1960s, and obviously an outing of some considerable size was being undertaken in what would have been luxury coaches of their day. The first coach is parked outside the very pleasant frontage of Faulkner and Alsop (Solicitors) and this was once Beethoven House, a music school. The following three coaches stand before Victor Value Supermarket and a very mundane block of offices. Only a few years earlier, however, this site had been occupied by the very fine Peacock Hotel, an old coaching inn, which was demolished in 1961. Strangely enough, the supermarket and office block in the photograph was itself bulldozed at a later date to make way for Peacock Place. Perhaps it should have been called Peacock's Revenge! The Market Square presents a motley collection of period vehicles in the photograph, including an A35 van, an A40 Farina and a Ford Anglia.

Plastered with adverts for whisky, baking powder and cocoa, the last of the town's horse drawn trams would make its way to the Phippsville terminus, near St Matthew's Church. Trams were first pulled by horses in Northampton in 1881. The first cars were single decker units operated by the Northampton Street Tramways Company. It was based in Abington Street where the Central Library now stands. It was now 1904 and the electrical age had arrived. Horsecar No 23 waited outside the Kingsley Park Hotel on the Kingsthorpe route. The conductor, E Patrick, and driver, W Hoskins, had already undergone a period of training to help them transfer to the new electric trams.

Considerably fewer Northamptonians will have participated in the training scheme for motorcyclists which was instituted in the early 1960s by the RAC and local clubs. The photograph shows one of the instruction sessions in progress, with the policeman on the right keeping a close watch on the trainees pedestrian crossing behaviour. The bikes themselves are of considerable interest and all of them now could be classed as period pieces. The police patrolman is astride a quite powerful looking BSA whilst, in contrast, the lady learner is aboard an LE Velocette, known as a 'noddybike'. Incredibly, although this scene pre-dated the compulsory wearing of crash helmets, nobody is wearing one, not even the policeman!

Interested onlookers wonder what is going on, as workmen paint white rectangles on the kerbs in Sheep Street, but in the war anything could happen! As soon as World War Two began, a general blackout was enforced so as to give enemy bombers no obvious targets. Householders could buy Lightproof Bolton Sheeting at 3s 11d (19p) per yard. More likely, they would buy rolls of blackout paper from Boots Chemists at 1s 6d (7p), or even fashion their own. The need for a total blackout was felt to be vital and it was common to hear the cry of, 'Put that light out!' from Air Raid Wardens patrolling the streets. Prosecutions for failing to observe the blackout were common. The problem was that at first a spate of accidents occurred in the densely black streets. Therefore local councils had to have such things as lamp-posts and kerbs painted, at least partially, in white.

Shopping Spree

Don't they know there's a war on? In spite of shortages and rationing, this busy Market Square scene from the early 1940s shows that people were determined to get out and see what they could snap up. And why not the luxury of some ice-cream? It would have to be Gallones of course, a household name in Northampton. The hidden benefit (not appreciated by 1940s housewives) was that shortages of sugar and fat, along with plenty of home-grown vegetables, meant that the diet of that day was probably healthier than that of today. There are some very distinctive marks of the 1940s on the photograph, not least the boneshaker prams and the sturdy Wolseley car with wartime headlight mask.

The long sweep of Sheep Street provides nothing more than an exercise in nostalgia now, for this row of small shops was demolished to provide a through road in conjunction with the Grosvenor Shopping Centre during 1971-72. This photograph was taken in 1963, and perhaps distance lends enchantment, but there seems to be something very attractive now about such a vista. The appeal lies in the variety of building styles and the different roof levels, partly the result of houses being turned into shops or extensions 'tacked on' at various times. Quite a few readers may remember these names that were once to be found on Sheep Street - Valentine Charles Ltd (wines and spirits); Frosts (children's shop); Sigwart's (with the pointing finger to help you). Last but not least was Ron's Wine, Beer and Coffee Tavern.

Left: It's a lively scene of human activity in the Market Square in the 1950s. The stalls are thronged and a hand-cart awaits to help unload the contents of the wagon marked 'Tomkins Seeds'. The handsome building outside which the wagon is parked is 'The Peacock'. This was an old coaching inn with stabling for 30 horses, a feature of the Square. As part of Northampton's heritage, it provided a link to the time when the horse was the speediest form of transport and the Market Square would echo to the sound of hooves and coach wheels on the cobbles. Unfortunately 'The Peacock' stood in the way of 1960s 'progress', a time when scant regard was given to continuity and tradition in the quest for modernity. This historic building was bulldozed in order to make way for a featureless office block in 1961.

Above: News had got around about certain items of clothing being off-ration and available for purchase without clothing coupons. Hence this gigantic queue at Lyons clothing shop on Mercers Row. This was, of course, the 1940s and the styles of dress on the photograph bear this out, as does the splendid tandem pram. It is difficult to envisage a time when you had only 66 coupons for clothes for a whole year, unless you lived through it. For a man, a shirt would set you back five coupons, trousers eight coupons and a jacket 13 coupons. Rationing on food was introduced early in 1940 and on clothing in June 1941.

A wonderful atmosphere of bustle and activity is evoked in this shot of Market Square showing an open-air market as it really should be. Masses of people are seeking that little bit of extra value for money, or even a real bargain, and you can almost hear the stallholders shouting out their special offers or exchanging banter with prospective customers. For many people in this photograph, the outing to market will have been not merely a shopping trip, but a social occasion, a chance to meet friends and have a gossip. Modern shopping centres have their advantages, but they seem anonymous and lifeless in comparison to the good oldfashioned open-air market. The busy scene pre-dates 1962, for that was the year in which the centre point of Market Square, the fountain, was dismantled. Some familiar names of the time may be seen on the premises in the background. On the left is Roses Fashion Centre in Waterloo House; then Phoenix Assurance; then Phelan and Agutter, Estate Agents. On the right-hand side of the Square the names of Pearl Assurance and Liptons are visible. The distinctive tower and cupola of All Saints Church dominates the skyline, with the dome of the Westminster Bank to the right.

Right: The 1960s Market Square shoppers perhaps took the backdrop of buildings for granted, unaware that soon all was to change. In 1972 this whole side of the Square was demolished to make way for the Grosvenor Centre, including the two buildings featured. To the left, the Emporium Arcade was a fine piece of Edwardian architecture, built in 1908, with an attractive two-toned frontage of bricks. The 1930s building to the right was home to Northampton's daily 'Chronicle and Echo' and the weekly 'Mercury and Herald.' This had been the site  of Northampton newspapers since the 1740s. The council's proposals to build a new shopping centre, and in so doing destroy fine buildings and historic links, met with fierce opposition.

Right: The clock on the Emporium Arcade stands at midday on a sunny Saturday in July 1966. Market Square presents a busy scene as the various stalls attract plenty of custom. The buildings to the rear give an impression of solidity and permanence, but within six years they were gone and this aspect of the Square had changed dramatically. With the buildings having been constructed at different times, each had its own stamp of individuality. Abel's Records, with the Pye logo beneath the name, was housed in a simple building that had been in business as a music shop since 1790. The Emporium Arcade, with its wonderful frontage of two-tone brickwork, had been erected in 1908.

At Work

Perched aloft on their scaffolding, these workmen are getting a close-up view which very few will have been able to enjoy. They may not be particularly appreciating the privilege, for it must have been hard work giving these Town Hall statues a wash and brush up, as captured in this photograph which dates back to the 1950s. Northampton Town Hall, the administrative heart of the town, was opened in 1863. It had been designed by Godwin, with extensions coming at later stages, the second section being designed by Matthew Holding. The building is noted for the wonderful carvings and statuary on its facade. These 14 life size statues, each with an elaborate canopy, represent famous figures from Northampton's history. They are truly beautiful examples of craftsmanship and it seems a pity that, for the most part, only the birds can regularly appreciate them at close quarters. The Town Hall is in good company, for just as impressive in its own way is the stately tower and cupola of All Saints Church in the background. Northampton can be proud of its 14 famous citizens, but it can also take great pride in the fine architecture which graces this part of the town.

The police sergeant looks as if he is giving the little boy a severe interrogation, but the kindly smile on the face of his colleague gives the game away. It is a case of a little boy lost and the constabulary coming to the rescue. This touching little scene was captured by Roland Holloway in George Row, near All Saints Church, in the 1930s. The day appears to be a chilly one, judging by the clothes on view, and the policemen in particular are well clad against the weather. They would have to be, for this was a time when most constables would be found pounding the pavement rather than in patrol cars - cold work in winter. A 'bobby on the beat', of course, had a good chance of picking up on a tearful toddler in distress whose expression gives every indication that he thinks the end of the world has come. Rescue was probably imminent, for apparently All Saints Church was a good place for mothers to be re-united with lost infants.

One year short of its centenary and the famous Market Square fountain has been felled. The scene is April 1962 and the cast-iron column, along with its four drinking bowls, its cattle troughs and its bronze decorations lies ready to be disposed of. The argument to justify this action was that the fountain had become fragile and dangerous. Nevertheless, it took a team of men, along with modern equipment, two days to get it down. The workmanship on this fragile Victorian treasure can clearly be seen on the photograph, and the men on the plinth are struggling with what appear to be the drinking bowls. The youngsters are enjoying all the excitement, but the action of the council caused an outcry locally. It seemed to many that this was wanton destruction of part of Northampton's heritage. A competition was held for the purpose of replacing the fountain. The winning entry was for a proposed structure to be named 'The Fountain of Light', by Willi Soukop, but it came to nothing.

It must have been a fine view of the centre of Northampton from up there, but a modern safety inspector would have a fit. The two workmen appear to be enjoying their ride on the huge bucket of bricks, but there is not a safety helmet in sight. Also, at some stage, the one with the cigarette in his mouth is going to have to cling on one-handed if he is actually going to smoke it! The date was 1946, and although there was little to be done in the way of repairing bomb damage, there was still improvement work on the menu. This particular scheme was concerned with demolishing the buildings that formed a bottleneck in Abington Street. The workers could enjoy the sight of some distinguished looking buildings from an unusual perspective. To the right, the fine looking building with the roof gables belonged to Doffmans. The succession of signs advertised the variety of their clothing operations - 'Showrooms'; 'Cutter and Fitter'; 'Resistorm Weathercoats'; 'Granby Rain-coats'; 'Ladies' Tailors'. This 1946 project was perhaps a straw in the wind' for the substantial redevelopment of the town centre in the 60s and 70s.

These boots are made for walking. If not just boots, then shoes as well. This was the closing room at Barratt's. Nearly all of those in this room were women. In those days, there was still a division between what was regarded as men's and women's work. The Barratt Boot and Shoe factory was in Kingsthorpe Road, designed by John Macvicar Anderson and opened in 1911. The company was one of the first to embrace the mail order business. A customer drew round his foot onto a piece of paper and sent the pattern to the appropriately named Footshape Works. The drawing was used to provide accurately fitting footwear. The firm continued to flourish into the mid-20th century under the advertising slogan "Walk the Barratt Way". Barratt's recognised its responsibility to the community, donating money for the building of a maternity home. The company became part of the Leeds based Stylo group in 1964.

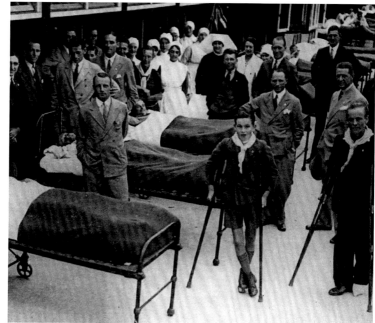

This was a memorable day for the Manfield Orthopaedic Hospital in 1930, and particularly for the boy scout troop which had been formed there that year. The notable visitors, who had come with the express purpose of giving a boost to the scouts, were members of the Australian cricketing tour party. The famous Don Bradman was amongst them. The Australian guests can be seen in the lighter suits, all looking very smart, and Bradman is in the foreground to the left. One of scouting's highest awards is to individual scouts who struggle successfully against adversity. In the case of these hospitalised scouts they surely all deserved the award. The two on crutches are proudly wearing their troop neckerchiefs and each has the scout badge in his lapel. Cricketing fans or not, they were probably thrilled to be meeting the 'Don' who, at 22, had become a legend already. Don Bradman was probably the greatest batsman of all time and perhaps his visit encouraged these scouts to even more determination.

The children of Stimpson Avenue School collect their Coronation souvenirs in June 1953.